The Book For T

The Book Woman Of Power

Lakita T. Sharpe

Copyright © Lakita T. Sharpe 2023

All rights reserved.

All rights reserved. No part of this book may be reproduced or transmitted in any form or by any means, electronic or mechanical, including photocopying and recording, or by any information storage and retrieval system, without permission in writing from the publisher.

Published in the United States by Lakita T. Sharpe. An imprint of Lakita T. Sharpe & Company

For Permission to use book in any way contact lakitatsharpebooks@gmail.com

www.lsharpe.simplesite.com

All fiction books are a product of the author's imagination. And people or any resemblance is just coincidental.

Lakita T. Sharpe's Signature Books

Lakita T. Sharpe's Books

Unstoppable: A Memoir; The Adventures of Rainbow Girl Series: Books 1-7; Hustle; Intense Love; What To Expect On Your Rise To Success; Lakita T. Sharpe's Successful Money Habits; How to Be A Successful Wife; How to Be A Successful Writer; How to Have Peace In Your Life; Lavish; How to Be A Successful Entrepreneur; From Burnout to Successful Girl Boss; A Hope That Was Lost; How to Make Your Husband Happy; The Happy Book; The Holiday Party; The Quarantine Party; How To Discover Your Dream; How to Gain Self-Confidence; How to Date Yourself; How to Create The Life You Envy; Envy; The Grocery Store; Overcoming Attacks: Being a Warrior In Christ; The Postman; Honk -Honk, Hi, Y'all I'm Leader Goose; How To Put Up With A Man You Hate; The Best Friends; Me And God Against The World; Becoming A Kingdom Woman; Girl Boss Rules: For The Female Entrepreneur; On The Road To Being A Millionaire; Chasing

Dreams: for The Lazy Person; Crown Yourself ; The Living Arrangement; Daddy's Girl; How To Be A Successful You; How To Set Your Mind Up For Entrepreneurship; Becoming a Millionaire You Series: Books 1,2,3; Freedom

Devotionals

- Lakita T. Sharpe's 365 Days of Godly Wisdom
- Lakita T. Sharpe's 31 Days of Devotion Books 1- 4

Journals

- Lakita T. Sharpe's Success Journal

There are more books available not listed.

Coach Yourself Books

-How to Discover Yourself, the Life Coach On The Go

Table of Contents

Title Page

Copyright

Lakita T. Sharpe Other Books

Dedication To Andre Chargois

Introduction

Chapter 1: The Woman of *Power*

Chapter 2: The Woman of *Power* That Excels

Chapter 3: A Woman of *Power* is No Ordinary Woman

Chapter 4: A Woman of *Power* is Magical

Chapter 5: A Woman of *Power* is Strong

Chapter 6: A Woman of *Power* is A Loving Woman

Chapter 7: A Woman of *Power* is Fierce

Chapter 8: A Woman of *Power* is Graceful Woman

Chapter 9: A Woman of *Power* is A Happy Woman

Chapter 10: A Woman of *Power* is A Blessed Woman

Chapter 11: A Woman of Power is A Selfless Woman

Chapter 12: A Woman of *Power* Pushes Through No Matter What The Circumstances

Chapter 13: A Woman Power Shines Through Darkness

Chapter 14: A Woman of *Power* Never Gives Up!

About The Author

Acknowledgements

Connect With Lakita T. Sharpe

Dedication

      I would like to dedicate this book to my brother Andre Chargois. He has been a supporter of *The Lakita T. Sharpe and Company.* He is a dedicated Christian and a wonderful and loving man of God of ministry. I have watched him grow from a young man into a flourished individual who is hardworking and takes care of his family and look after people who are less fortunate.

      He is a notable example of exemplifying what a "Man of God" should be. He has Godlike qualities such as generosity, kindness, and a loving soul.

      Andre Chargois is and forever will be a staple in the *Lakita T. Sharpe & Company Ministry family.* I salute Mr. Chargois for his Presence in the military as well as his Presence in the Holy Kingdom of God.

      Please take this time and acknowledge his kindness in helping me bring this project to life.

      I thank you for being a part of this ministry, Paster Andre Chargois. Blessings to you and your family.

Forever love,

Your sister,

And sister in Christ,

Lakita T. Sharpe

Lakita T. Sharpe 11/27/2023

Introduction

This book represents the woman of *Power*. The woman who has been through a lot in life. The woman who has endured so much to get to where she is today.

This book speaks about who the woman of *Power* is and what she is made out of.

This book is a contribute to the woman of *Power* in your life or if you are that woman of *Power*.

This book will be a reminder to keep going no matter what comes your way! And that winter doesn't last forever because a woman of *Power* is the Sun and shines bright through darkness. She carries the light of Power.

Chapter 1

The Woman of *Power*

"For The Spirit God gave us does not make us timid, but gives us power, love and self-disciplined. "2 Timothy 1;7

    The woman of *Power* has been given power and authority to be who God has called her to be. She is a woman who knows who she is. She is a woman who is a person who believes in her own Power. She carries herself in a way that exemplifies truth and honor. She walks with her head held high.

A woman of *Power* is a woman of standard. She doesn't just settle for anything that comes her way. She gives everything a long thought and consideration. She is deliberate with everything.

A woman of *Power* doesn't just sit around and wait for things to happen. She makes things happen. She knows that her actions is what going to bring her long-term success.

She is a business minded woman. She keeps herself busy by doing the things she loves and what she is called to do.

A woman of *Power* is not an easy woman. She is a woman who takes care of herself and has high quality and standards for herself and her family.

This woman is favored by God, the most high.

She is loved, treasured, and valued by the most high God.

She has favor everywhere she goes she is a chosen woman. Check out the book I've written titled ""When God Chooses You" sold at Amazon.com

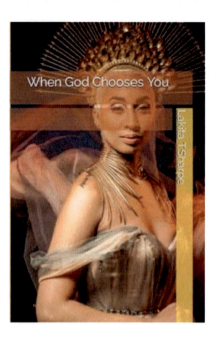

The woman of *Power* is a well-kept woman. She knows who she is. She manages her household well. She lifts up her home and does not tear it down. She is a good woman and not a bad woman. She is a woman of quality.

The woman of *Power* is a drama-free woman because she knows her place. She knows that her image is everything and maintaining an image of peace, and having substance to her character.

A woman of a *Power* is an elegant woman. A woman of grace. A woman who ages backwards. She is timeless and flawless. She is a Great woman. She is a designer woman. A unique woman in her own right.

This woman of *Power* has a cleanliness about her.

She is a woman who is free to be herself. She is a Golden butterfly. A "golden butterfly" is a woman of standard, and quality. She's incredibly special and has transformed from a low quality to the highest made quality. She's pure.

A woman of "Power" most of all is classy. Check out my book at Amazon.com "How to be Classy Human Barbie Doll by Being Yourself."

This book is for teaching a woman how to be a classy woman who represents Barbie. Barbie is a woman of *Power* in her own right. She stands for entrepreneurship. A woman in business.

Chapter 2

The Woman of *Power* That Excels

Excellence. What is the spirit of excellence? A person with an excellent spirit always does things differently. He is not looking out for short cuts but is willing to do things right no matter the sacrifice it entails. To manifest the spirit of excellence is to be highly organized and live an orderly life.

In the bible God gave Daniel a spirit of excellence. He was preferred above the presidents and princes, because an excellent spirit was in him over the whole realm. All throughout the society in which we live, excellence is rewarded. Everyone is looking for someone who is excellent at something.

It pays to be a woman of *Power* with an excellent spirit. She will be set high above anyone else and will be chosen out of many for a job well done. She will be honored by God and society.

There are many people in the world who have shown a spirit of excellence. Some of my favorites are Joyce Meyers, Condoleezza Rice, Michelle Obama, Oprah Winfrey, Sarah Jakes Roberts, Priscilla Shirer, Valorie Burton, Jennifer Hudson, The YouTube Star, Pretty Boss TV, The You Tube Star, Bella Bashan, The YouTube Star, The Mindset Elevator, Beyonce, The YouTube Star, Cristi Jesses, The YouTube Star, Shonda Inspires, The YouTube Star, Jordan Journey, The YouTube Star, Daniella Oyaga, Serita Jakes, Kamala Harris, Danielle Steel writing so many books. Michelle Williams, Rosalee Barnes, my mother, Beyonce's Mother, Tina Knowles. I'm sure there are other women out there that are women of *Power*. But these women are the ones who has touched me in some way.

A woman of excellence is a branded woman. She owns her style and her walk. She is professionally managed and put together. She is organized. And well prepared.

A woman of excellence is professionally qualified to get the things she wants and deserves from God because he knows her heart.

Her heart posture is what truly makes her a woman of excellence.

Chapter 3

A Woman of *Power* is No Ordinary Woman

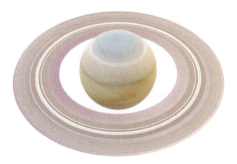

When we look at the word ordinary. Ordinary means with no special or distinctive features; normal. When God created the woman of "Power" he created her with unique features which makes her extraordinary. Extraordinary means very unusual or remarkable. Synonyms: exceptional, wonderful, astonishing, unbelievable, miraculous, phenomenal, spectacular.

You as a woman of "Power" are all those things and more.

There is nothing ordinary about you. You have what it takes to be who you want to be. You have the magic that makes you wonderful in every way.

You are unique in your own way. Can't anybody do it the way you do it! You have your own style, your own way of doing things. You are great and awesome in all your ways.

When you touch something, it becomes gold. No matter what you do it will be a success!

You will be a bestselling author! The successful coach! The greatest business owner and Powerhouse. A bestselling real estate agent! Or insurance agent! You will be the successful head nurse! The successful nail technician and cosmetician. The Successful chef! The amazing homemaker. And whatever you put your mind to. You are that extraordinary! And awesome.

God has even given you an extraordinary name.

Yes, it was meant to be different.

I want to share a short story with you. There was a time that I used to look at my name and I didn't see anything special about it. In fact, I didn't feel as confident about who I was. In my adult life when I became married and changed my name to Lakita T. Sharpe, God had plans for that name. I eventually grew into the knowledge of me being who God has destined for me to be. The more I became aware of my destiny and working on my business I saw my name as something great! I began to feel differently about my name. It was no longer a low name but a high-class name.

I am here to say that God is making your name Great! Your name will be famous among nations. I will bless you. I will make you famous and a blessing to others. Genesis 12:2-3

Everyday you wake up God will be renewing you. You will have an extra dose of happiness, love, peace, creativity, awesomeness and more.

Yes, he is feeling you up with extraordinary things.

Chapter 4

A Woman of *Power* is Magical!

A woman of *Power* is a magical woman. She is a woman that knows what she wants in life. She is a woman who can make things happen by her faith. She is a woman that can do anything that she puts her mind to. She is a good woman.

A woman of *Power* can move anything around when she uses her imagination. She knows that her dreams come true from just imagining what she wants to see what happens. She imagines herself in a new home, a new car, a new relationship etc. She sees the possibilities in all she does.

She is a good woman that is on fire. A woman of action. She doesn't just announce it, she accomplishes it.

She's magical in all her ways and she is attractive and distinct in her own way.

She is that magical.

Chapter 5

A Woman of *Power* is Strong

A woman of *Power* is strong. A woman of *Power* takes care of herself. A woman of *Power* does what she needs to do to be able to survive. A woman of

"Power" is a great woman. She can handle a lot of things that come her way.

Life may have done things to get her down and to try to steal her confidence, but she was able to bounce back and be who she is meant to be.

She's fantastic and resilient.

Anything that happens to her she takes it and uses it for her good and creative purposes.

A woman *Power* is an ideal woman that people inspire to be such as her friends, family, colleagues, and children and even her spouse secretly admires her. She is a trusted woman.

She knows how to keep secrets.

Chapter 6

A Woman of *Power* is A Loving Woman

A woman of *Power* is a loving woman. She is a woman that is loving in all her ways. Sometimes people may take advantage of lovingness and kindness. She loves people and is genuine in her ways.

God is moved by her very essence because of her loving soul.

Her husband loves it. Her children adore her and her pets. And the world admires her.

The woman of *Power* is loving but don't cross her because she will let you know that she isn't the one to be played with.

A woman of *Power* stands tall, bright, and confident in all her ways.

Chapter 7

A Woman of *Power* is Fierce

A woman of *Power* is a fierce woman. She is unstoppable. She is unmovable. She is a baddy! She is successful in every way and destined to win in life.

She has a mindset to change the game. She is a cocreator with God.

A woman of *Power* says that I can do all things! She is the boss of her world.

She is the boss!

Check out my book "The True Boss Lady" Sold at Amazon.com

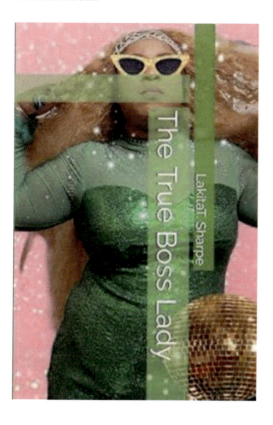

Chapter 8

The Woman of *Power* is A Graceful Woman

A woman of *Power* is a graceful woman. Graceful means elegance. She is elegant in her way and classy! She stands for something magnificent.

She is a true beauty.

An original piece of art!

She is a mogul.

She is neither black nor white. She is who she is.

She is full of spices and all the right ingredients.

She is sensual.

She doesn't allow fear to stop her in any way.

Chapter 9

A Woman of *Power* is A Happy Woman

A woman of *Power* is a happy woman. She is a woman that knows what she wants and is content.

She's filled with joy and has a good heart.

She loves to smile.

She loves to talk and share the goodness of her life.

She's humbled in every way but yet she is great!

A woman of *Power* is happy because she can be herself without making excuses.

She can be her authentic self and show up in the world correctly.

A woman of *Power* shines bright in every way!

She has what it takes to constantly make it to the next level of her life.

She is advancing in every way!

Chapter 10

A Woman *of Power* is A Blessed Woman

A woman of *Power* is a blessed woman. She is a woman who is fearless, powerful and have the backings of God with her everywhere she goes. When she goes to a place such as a store or an outing people stare at her. She gets attention everywhere she goes.

She is a good woman. An exceptionally good woman.

The favor of God travels with her everywhere she goes.

She is never alone.

She is blessed and highly favored.

The universe works in her favor.

Chapter 11

The Woman of *Power*

is a Selfless Woman

A woman of *Power* is a selfless woman. She is a woman who put others first. She always thinks of others, and she is generous. She is good at a lot of things. She is well educated. She is well grounded. She is a brilliant woman.

She always thinks of others.

She does good and not harm.

She is full of creativity and body!

She is awesome in every way.

Chapter 12

A Woman of Power Pushes Through No Matter What The Circumstances

A woman of *Power* pushes through no matter what the circumstances. She can go through sicknesses, face hardships, and experience difficulties but she will find herself pushing herself through whatever she is going through.

She has the backings of God who is helping and giving her the strength to push forward and move ahead.

That's why she is a powerful woman because things come to knock her down, but she always finds her way to push forward and to move ahead.

She is a good woman.

A woman that people admire everywhere she goes and people want to be like.

Chapter 13

A Woman of *Power* Shines Through The Darkness

A woman of *Power* shines through the darkness. She can be experiencing a dark season, but yet she still rises through all her trouble. She will work herself out of the darkness and smile her way out until she looks back and find herself enjoying one of her best seasons.

A woman of *Power* will shine no matter what she goes through she will come out on top every time.

A woman of *Power* is always doing her thing and being a blessing to many.

She will never stay in the dark because she was meant to shine through it all.

She is brilliant like the sun. And people need her to stay alive. She is awesome in all her ways.

No one will ever be able to put her light out unless she gives them that Power to do so.

She will always shine bright like the sun!

She gives life and energy to everyone she meets.

Chapter 14

A Woman of *Power* Never Gives Up!

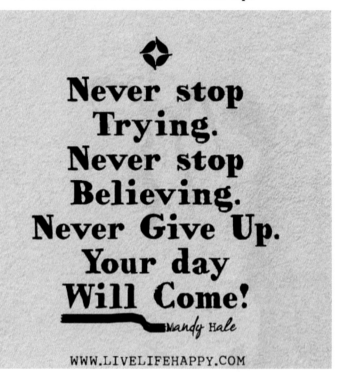

Jasmine, The Tiger >>>>"Be Brave ,Strong, and Courageous!" God, Deuteronomy 31:6

A woman of Power never gives up or loose hope. A woman of Power will fight for her life, and she will do all she can do to make it to the top of where she suppose to be. She is full of courage.

God is with her, and she cannot fail. She will fight to the very end of her life and won't let go!

She is awesome in all her ways. No matter what she does and what comes against her, to attack her. She remains strong and she fights.

She may cry many times and tears may roll down her eyes even when she is doing her business or just hanging out!

She may hide sometimes and cry out to God, but she keeps trucking knowing that the Creator has more for her life.

She gets scared, and she wants to give up sometimes, but she knows that many people are counting on her to help them get back up!

When she cries her tears mean so much to God her tears aren't ordinary tears.

Her tears are powerful tears and heaven listens to her pain, sorrow, and moans.

So much has come up against her and sometimes she feels like she is going to break at any minute. She has experienced losses in her life. She has been through so much and even abuse has come her way. She experienced so much tragedy.

Sometimes she feels so alone. The enemy hates her, but yet loved by God and others.

She is becoming stronger and stronger by the day because she continues to keep going no matter what has come her way.

She hurts, she has pain. She is tired at times for doing her best most of the time.

She is a dedicate woman and she dedicated to what she believes in.

Sometimes she just cries out. Life has been tough for her.

She knows she deserves a good life. A life to be admired by many.

There are many women in the world, but the woman of Power is one who stands by herself!

She is a woman that could never stay down when the enemy tries to knock her down.

A woman *Power* will live for time, and she will be celebrated and praised for years to come. She deserves it all and whatever her heart desires.

About The Author

Lakita T. Sharpe is a woman of *Power* who resides in Portsmouth, Virginia with her loving cat, Jasmine.

Lakita T. Sharpe is the author of over one hundred books.

Lakita T. Sharpe loves wisdom, success, and creativity.

Acknowledgements

I would like to thank God for giving me this idea that popped into my head one night. I would like to thank his Holy Spirit for helping me write this book that was emotional for me.

I would like to thank my husband for his support when he can.

I would like to thank my parents for giving me life. Vernon Kitabu Turner, Rosalee Barnes and Joyce Turner, my bonus mother.

I would like to thank my cat, Jasmine, for all the love and the comfort she gives me just by being here at night with me. She hasn't left my side since the day I got her other than when we were separated at one time.

I would like to thank my readers. I love my readers and I need them. You picking up this book is important to me and having you near just knowing someone on the other side comforts me. Thanks, my

Diamond!

Connect with Lakita T. Sharpe

 @ Lakita T. Sharpe

 Authoress_lakita_t_sharpe

YouTube   The Adventures of Rainbow Girl Series Book Ministry

Website: www.lsharpe.simplesite.com

Email: Lakitatsharpebooks@gmail.com

To Sow into this ministry:

www.paypal.me/lakitatsharpe

CashApp/$LakitaTSharpe

Venmo/ @LakitaTSharpe

For **Private Coaching** Services reach out to my website and use the contact form

www.lsharpe.simplesite.com

Made in the USA
Middletown, DE
04 May 2024